A Broken Bowl

A Broken Bowl

PATRICK FRIESEN

Brick Books

CANADIAN CATALOGUING IN PUBLICATION DATA

Friesen, Patrick, 1946-
A broken bowl

Poems.
ISBN 0-919626-93-9

I. Title.

PS8561.R496B76 1997   C811'.54   C97-930819-4
PR9199.3.F74B76 1997

We acknowledge the support of the Canada Council for the Arts
for our publishing programme. The support of Ontario Arts Council
is also gratefully acknowledged.

The author wishes to thank the Manitoba Arts Council.

The cover and interior photographs
are by Marijke Friesen and Pedro Mendes.

The typeface is Galliard,
and the stock is acid-free Zephyr Antique laid.
Printed and bound by The Porcupine's Quill Inc.

Brick Books
431 Boler Road, Box 20081
London, Ontario, N6K 4G6

I 2 3 4 • 99 98 97

⊠

rain comes down
all night
slopping over the eaves

toward morning
it slows
into long silences
broken by air
shifting
shaking drops down
leaf to leaf

before light
the world fills
with birds

their song
their fine ancient bones

✖

the river is a filthy transfusion it's what the doctor ordered a last disease
I'm watching my slow heart attack feeling the pain and the love
maybe this is how it all began how it was meant to go the boyish heart
  giving up
song is the plasma that flows through the world a map of my body before
  it turns away

someone's fishing off the bridge there's a silver hook a lovely hook
 dangling above the river and the sun's glittering on stones and water
 and the air so soft it feels like old days
someone's singing on the bridge some swan song some courting ballad
 a round song someone's singing hymns
there's a rustling of leaves and the bushes shiver as shadows emerge
 shuffling to the shore
their eyes their glassy eyes fastened on the hook their eyes begin to
 glisten with yearning and love

listen I've been dreaming gypsies I've spent long nights at their fires I've
 been tattooed and wooed I've been had

I've danced with the rose of sharon

�֍

reading webster's violence and anarchy
even the stars collapsing in mad ping pong
thumb screws and the rack brass knuckles the knife and chain
yeah the story the split skull the slithering brain
animal lashing out taking care of its own
and the *fuck you* human full of rage the imagination on automatic fear
the deliberation of torture and spot-check violence
I cause pain and death therefore I am
mind and body brought together by pain
human distance is an awful thing

⊗

an ancient violence is tearing the doors from their hinges
the people in their despair let loose long memory
like a terrible freedom the hawk plunging down

an ancient democracy
ancient violations

what's left is the foddering of children and the business of love

�֍

you were asking about the mess fools through the centuries blind as kings
fools in their garb and glamour their genuflections and honour fools on
st. bartholomew's day with their stations of the cross

you were wondering about the lottery the boat almost no one caught easy
street the moments and turning points the small births and tangents

the ruthless deviations of time in the bone

�֎

this is a dead man
dead dead dead
this is a man with feet
a man puzzled in the marsh
with its red-winged blackbirds
its reeds and frogs
this is a man with his feet sinking in dreams
a man devoured by the world
and how he missed it

✖

hallucinations of the cave
scattered with broken skulls and bones
what's left ten thousand years after the feast
grandpa and uncle willie and aunt trish
snacking on each other to get them through the age

⊗

the executioner's silhouette
his relentless arm his stance and his hidden eyes
he measures his victim
notices a stray hair on the shoulder
his victim half-turns to blow it away
they want nothing

✷

it's taking forever
but I'm learning to speak
once again

I've begun to beg
I've got nothing but pride
and that's just what I've got to shake

it's always last things

father's in the cellar
building a sailing ship
mother's in the attic
humming *white christmas*

children looking down the well
and wishing on a star

�֍

not enough lies to fill the day
not enough deceptions to know a truth

a red-winged blackbird swaying on a reed in the ditch isn't very much
  among the broken glass and papers in greasy swampwater near
  kokomo road
but it's something a splash of blood a clear song a dream a memory it's
  something left behind forgotten something to hear in the morning's
  first light
a haunting a ghost this is how god and darwin dance this song of world
  this echo of northern lights and marsh
it's something entering your eyes and ears and skin an invisible tattoo
  a braille you feel and read but nothing revealed

it's me remembering how I saw the bird on its reed everything changes
  in the looking

scavengers on the outskirts
with their drums and bracelets
the ones with no claims
and long memories

buying bullets with an unemployment cheque
shooting rats and listening to them squeal
living in a chevvy or a ford
history is bunk it isn't real

shooting pedestrians from a car
what are cars for? and guns?
shooting shadows in windows
watching them fall

�֍

living in the horrible dream running and running in slow motion or no
motion at all and gasping for breath and my heart exploding in its cage
living in static and panic in paralysis living in dread knowing the absence
of will knowing and running and gasping with a faceless fear
knowing this is a dream is not a dream knowing it's all in my hands and I
can't find them and I can't turn my head I would do anything to wake

if someone reached out touched me hand on arm flesh and flesh if
someone crossed the border and shook me awake a shout a violence
if someone came to earth on wings a hawk a vulture if someone saw me
frozen in my running and flew to me talons on my shoulder a beak a
waking pain
if someone screamed a murderous scream a cry of anguish if someone
slaughtered the dead air around me if I screamed and woke myself to
the world

this memory begins with brown thistles in an overgrown cemetery with
  broken stones looking like loaves of bread in the long grass
that's what I remember as I begin as I intend to write the poem to find the
  words that will say something concerning a disintegrating world I love

�֍

a bag woman
in the cold nights
water lapping at her feet
her hunger
among the spoils
her frozen body
there is no bliss
nothing is learned

⌀

the attic reaching for the sky

a dead dove in the poisonous eave

sloshing through the flood downstairs
broken walls and rainfall

trying to build a river

the river beneath the river

✖

walking past the school
with its million mirrored windows
with its flagpole
with its iron door
and I can't see anyone
through the fractured panes
and no one's singing

⊠

there's a suicide on the sill
a brown shadow in the afternoon
beneath him in the streets
the lemmings run for the sea
with newspapers cheering them on
the politicians waving
as they step into their black limousines

✖

one foot in front of the other
neither leaving nor entering
on the way

like romanovs they assume God's grace
a sacred permission to move in splendor
to guide a helpless people

evenings in the scented mauve boudoir

heard some inarticulate rage
stilettos in the nursery
bombs for cocktail hour
where arrogance sits on the throne

what keeps me going
not knowing
the next moment
the possibilities of world
its pleasure
and horror
what keeps me from my own hand
the questions question
curious boy in his tree
sniffing thin air
for the next scent
for the ascent

✹

it is impossible to be good
only shame and desolation move in the world
only betrayal and rage

this city does not have enough history
we have not yet learned the assassin's hopelessness

a child on two pillows
peering over the dash of a stolen car
a hammer on his lap

single mother with her knife
a shotgun in grannie's mouth
the babysitter puts a match to the block

someone got screwed in the alley
seems like a party
butt-ends and lysol
a fiddler playing the hopeless polka
everyone staggering arm-in-arm
looking for the government

always drums from the first heart beating to feet slapping hard earth the
   world over hands clapping the lost human finding a door the crack of a
   drum and entering earth's rhythm the cave of bones the path through the
   heart and beyond

the human infection spreading like music

I no longer sing the lullabyes
no longer remember the melodies or the words

tongue confounded
the world scattered with grammar
we listen for the song

what I have today
a son and daughter
a striped sweater
blue shorts
my hands in my pockets
fingering $53.56 and safarik's house key
and I have my bare feet

suicide as the final question
the only question left
the person
or the race
turning and going back

⊗

I'll say whatever you want that the river is rolling with heads I'll say I've haunted highways with a blade I've sliced a fetus from its womb and nailed a lizard to a tree I've lived in doorways heard lovers through the walls I'll say whatever you want and it's the truth I'll say whatever you want there are no fingerprints

I am the phone call you dread the filthy words the pain you hide behind your pills I am your mother with her guilt your father with his amnesia

I am your divinity the monster you dream at night I am who you want to be free with a pocketful of gold I am your leader I speak from the throne

this is not a confession this is a treatise on love this is your religion your philosophy of life this is how you make truth

I will tell you who I am I will tell you who you are

✖

*I was there at the tournaments with galahad and gawain in the midst of
all the stories the treachery the restlessness of hearts I paused at calvary
watching the shifting skies I played rome in the back alleys and beneath
bridges I passed through byzantium and baghdad travelled along the silk
road I was there in darkest africa with the missionaries in dublin on the
banks of the liffey in paris in budapest well you name it like the song goes
'I've been everywhere'*

*you can call me Mr. Love the Prince of Love whatever you want I am love
and can tell you about love I can tell you whoever said you must sacrifice
your self for love is wrong dead wrong*

*you must sacrifice your self to love that is the only way on your knees at the
altar of love*

I am what you want the hook and you are the fish that is love

*I am love in a smoky room I light a cigarette with hands cupping a flame
hands touching in a momentary transaction there are a dozen ways for my
hands to move a thousand seductions*

*I am love in the kitchen with my endless demands for perfection I am love
that throws dishes at the walls I tell you love is in the crumbs and shards on
the floor and you will learn me well on your knees*

*I am love in the medicine cabinet with bottles of magic I am love during
the long night when you sit on the edge of the white bathtub with a fistful of
death where would you be without me?*

*I am love in the boredom of the bedroom I am the love that forces your legs
apart when you are half-asleep the love that works hard to build a recalci-
trant erection I am the love child you will never make I am the love
revulsed by a partner growing old with lines around the lips with hair in
the ears and nose with hanging flesh on the arms and wattles beneath the
chin I am love in the sanctity of mutual disgust and grudge and routine*

I am love with each rape in the alley or in a penthouse suite I am love in violence and assault I hold the camcorder for the family gathering

I am love in church in the bible and in tricks turned in the back room I am love where the stained collar bends down to screw his secretary yes I am great love in the service of the lord

I am the aphrodisiac of power I bring love to cabinet ministers in their locked offices at night I am the love of a quickie beneath the desk the love of greed and power I am the love that makes little nameless men in suits feel important and righteous how else to be governed?

I am the ultimate love I am satisfaction today I am the satiation of greed and the itch give yourself to love give your freedom to this hook this aching need you have I will always be the right love for you the one that scratches your itch again and again and you'll return over and over again and haven't I always given you what you want?

※

I'm a policeman in a honda or a volkswagen with windows rolled down and headlights doused lurking at dark streetcorners or turning slowly into alleys silently inching along between windowless walls looking for the children huddled beneath newspapers or cardboard boxes rifles bristling from the windows a spotlight playing along the walls something moves a child wipes at his eyes rises from his sleep a broken blade in his hand and meets the bullets with his boney chest

I am justice the exterminator doing what you are unable to do but what you want me to do your beliefs intact and your outrage safe in your warm home

✼

I am the law of the land the liturgy of wealth and power the law with its underbelly and its shadows the law that fools you into civilization the law that steals from the ancient people and proclaims the thieves innocent the law the law that is the paperwork of the victors

and I am the other law that turns on the law tooth and claw the law of human rage in its tatters and torn shoes the law of serf and slave of the poor and the damaged and the brown and black the law of the human spirit misshapen by law I am the hidden river bursting its banks the law that passes understanding the law of the cornered rat and the insane child beneath the bridge

I am the law that turns on the righteous and greedy and narrow I am the law that puts a blade into the hand of the broken and sick and hopeless I am the law that strings up the tyrant and becomes the new one

everywhere I am the law everywhere and I favour none all will die beneath the law judged judged judged

✖

what do you want to hear on your birthday?

I can tell you how beautiful you are in body and spirit I can tell you that you are loved and admired and respected that you are worthwhile and life would be poorer without you

I can tell you that your loneliness is a vigil that will soon end that you have been tempered in the fire of despair and earned rewards in heaven

I can tell you that your numbed body will be awakened tonight that you will be ridden all night by the most gorgeous godly creature of your fantasies that you will be satiated and fall into the sleep of the well-fucked I can tell you that in the morning you will remember nothing and be free

I can tell you that God sees you and Jesus weeps for you that the Buddha smiles on you that all the saints and prophets pray for you in heaven I can tell you that you will be reborn and life will be sweet and full and joyful that there will be no returning to the old skin and old habits

I can tell you anything and as always I will that's why I'm here your only friend your confidante your lover in a riven world

I can tell you the truth I am the one that makes truth I am the truth as long as you tell me what you want to hear on your birthday as long as you call on me in the deep of your night

�֎

the stillness I've waited for ... that's been gone so many years from this land ... the stillness behind the cacophony of radio, of airplanes and streets, the braying of loud lies from governments, the noise of commerce on land, sea and air, of sport and culture, the sounds of our desperate busyness, our forgetting ... who would have thought when it all inevitably slowed down, that the stillness would be so empty, so terrible, rubble in the alley, burned-out buildings, thistles in the city, rats and vomit, the great vacancy...

reading newspapers
between the lies
information horoscopes and ads
and an endless fascination
for the lurid deaths of stars and saints

greasy newspapers
holding fat fish or hocks or steak

newspapers blowing about in the streets
fluttering against the grate on a basement window
scraping down an alley at 3 a.m.

newspapers for beds
rustling beneath bridges
shining in the full moon
beside the assiniboine

⊗.

who the hell knows how these things happen? ... it's not the strangest sight I've seen ... still, I can't think of an explanation for it ... here, on the banks of the assiniboine, not far from the writhing statue of louis riel ...

a pair of shoes ... and pants and a shirt lying around them ... as if someone just drifted out of his shoes and floated away, pants and shirt falling down on the shoes ...

it's a filthy place, all shit, used condoms, punctured lysol cans, and the smell of rotting flesh ... still, I'm thinking, he got away ... a kind of resurrection ... unexplained grace ... some drunk or chicken hawk ... someone with heroin veins ... some unlucky saint ...

scum by name
all filth and smell
oily tangled hair
a torn coat slippery with grease
scum by name
asleep on the steps
of an osborne village shop

scum as cliche
it's all been said and thought
a social question
a matter of economics and mental health
it's all been writ
blah blah blah

scum
assault on the senses
embarrassment disgust
a shame
shit no one wants to step in

greasy outline on the sidewalk
body on the riverbank
river turning to swamp
a fetid cesspool

riverbank's swarming with dogs
a dalmation looking for a fire
a poodle going for a haircut
and they smell the stench
the blood and filth and puke
they find them there
among the newspapers and bottles
they find them
sprawled blue flesh

with its spittle and stubble
the glory of the simple life
and laughter bloody right
they find them at the riverside
and tear them to shreds of meat
like lions in the serengeti
yes nature having its way
the night alive with snarls and laughter
and wildlife photographers
this is how things are meant to be
and darwin rests easy
his smile the grimace of putrefaction
lips drawn back
teeth black with blood
this how it goes this bliss
fuckall forever and ever amen
this is how

this century's poems
conjuring words
names and places
sarajevo
auschwitz
soweto
these incantations
like train cars clicking by
or convoys rolling through rubble
dubrovnik
mogadishu
hiroshima
like parachutes drifting through a summer sky
or fireworks
or a million footsteps
solovetzki
watts
kanewake
a million footsteps
leading to the river
the baptism
kings and princes on the barge
dancing with the whores
listening to water music
and playing die

shooting rats on dead-end street
listening to them squeal
baby clothes drying on the line
cut the cards and deal

there's a brain tumour in the house
a lung in the microwave

I'm reading daddy's sermons on the roof
momma's singing along with george beverley shea

the walls are crawling with melanoma
it's sunday every day

someone throw me a cobalt bomb
someone feed my x-ray

heading for jerusalem
or someplace holy

the distance of highways
their catastrophic scenes

the musician tearing
strings from his guitar

the doctor and the lawyer
priests of the unborn and the dying

priestesses clawing at their own faces
looking for divinity

death of a bag lady
huddled beneath the bridge

a faceless queer
floating down the assiniboine

an old man without memory
hanging from a tree

death of a rat
crawling into the river

shots echoing from the hill
broken glass on the lawn

a fiddler's playing polkas
and dancing on the black star

someone with a kitchen knife
is looking for the government

✖

the alarm drills through my head
my eyes fly open uncomprehending
when I finally invent myself my circumstances
I throw aside my blanket and lurch into a sitting position
the floor is cold on my feet
I look down and see an old man's stick legs
my invented self falls away into the black hole of memory
and though it's the beginning of a new day
I have to laugh

☒

scattered photos beneath the bridge
a rag doll and a bottle in a paper bag

who's been sleeping here?

momma's gone for a minute
kettle's on for tea
she'll be back soon
I know she loves me

photos of someone's kid
children of the golden arch
shit-kicking children of the knife

fuck you fuck you fuck you!
yeah that's my girl

daddy's in the cellar
building a sailing ship
mother's in the attic
humming *white christmas*

⊠

jostled and harangued
along city walls
feet blinded by the streets

rats raping each other
on dead-end road

radio blasting from a window
GLORIA
an evangelist shouting in the park
holy fuck ma we're all going to hell

a woman's laying on hands she's got the heat
one-eyed cats three-legged dogs and a world of cancer

a virgin crawling through the station
her boy's coming home on the midnight special

everyone wants something
that doesn't have a name

GLORIA

✠

the city sucks
I'm feeling fucked over
the latest in a long line
of ancestors
born with all their baggage
and civilization
who wouldn't want to shriek?

I need smack
the pain never leaves
a million voices jangling
ejaculating
everyone on everyone's feet
rats creeping along the foundation
everyone's cooking in my face
everyone's breath
and nowhere to turn

the city sucks
and I'm puking on the street
sick to my heart
scratching to get out of the shoebox
running up and down alleys
to find some cheese
I want to feel nothing
know no one
sitting on a broken wall
watching the traffic flow away

newspapers caught in a wrought-iron fence
the usual broken glass and needles
a child crying from a window
the street turns golden in the afternoon
someone's having it out across the street
you can see their angry silhouettes
humans cursing each other
they must be in love

the city sucks
everything's fucked
flowers plucked
gotta have some smack
someone hit me
someone give me a dream
a second birth
jesus saves jesus saves
all I want is to shake off the baggage
someone climb out of the fucking tree
and take my place
it's a long way back
and I'm tired
but it's somewhere to go

someone throw me a cobalt bomb
someone heal my x-ray

mama's on her knees
she's got you in her prayers

convulsions behind the wall
this is not a good day

crawling into a bottle of booze
looking for ma
looking for the end of a rainbow
looking for what passes understanding

crawling into bed
looking for forgetfulness
looking for comfort
looking for a mirror

crawling into church
looking for pa
looking for oblivion
looking for the third day

crawling into jesus' arms
looking for a brother
looking for a laugh
looking for the bullet

crawling into the cave
looking for the stone
looking for the word
looking for home

⊗

father's crawling into bed
ma's coughing behind the door

billy graham's saving souls on radio
mickey mantle's winning the triple crown

got strapped in the basement
I'm kicking the furnace and cursing God

✖

no salvation
we just dig ourselves deeper
with each attempt
there is only this
walking and crawling and standing still
there is only this victim this murder
there is the human hand on a shovel
digging for clues

I am the words flowing by words and words and words from politicians and business people from poets from children's singers and actors from novelists from preachers and teachers from interest groups doctors administrators minorities disabled words and words and words

I am the words that boil in a cauldron looking for magic for paradise for wealth and happiness boiling with a poisonous steam boiling away all meaning all truth all life

I am words flowing by like a filthy river ideologies and theories and postures words words words while the world goes down

✗

I am the black dog that follows you home that sleeps beneath the lilac hedge until the sun rises the dog that pauses in a shadow while you stop to reconsider your life the black dog that terrorizes you in a dream

✖

*everything is good look around everything is a silver lining there is nothing
else*

*that baby in the stroller twisting back to see her tall mother the mother's
dark hair windswept across her face dry leaves rattling along the sidewalk.
you've known this moment forever*

murders in the newspaper torture floods you know this too

all is good I tell you the truth

for a moment

⊗

in the heat of july
the deep sadness of the moon landing
a heavy foot floating down the ladder
into the fine dust of gods

a preacher's cliche for history
and spinoza groaning in his sleep

�҈

we are romans with our headaches and anxiety we are a trivial people
  brutish and blind
we are romans standing in sewage craving the law and God with his
  scalene triangle
senators and patricians spread their greed and flash to the eager plebs
  and we run to the arena
there is murder in the streets hostages and spectators strippers become
  naked again and again
there is such a thirst for another city unquenchable a thirst for some rich
  city a walled place of desire
but all cities are rome the boutiques and love shops and the buildings of
  law and order

we are romans with our senators our laws and our shabby gods we
  worship everything nothing is sacred

the bronze horseman rides alone
in his terrible intelligence
once more through mist and rain
back to the northern bog

this is how you build a city
on the bones of ghosts
you wrench a civilization
out of the silences of history

this is how you satiate kings
how you obey the mob
you fashion paradise with terror
and worship angels in the beast

emperor
romanov at dominoes and patience in the mauve boudoir
as dying armies march across the maps of europe
romanov
diffident in his greatcoat and boots
dazed and uncomprehending

sons and daughters raging on the streets
armies bloodying the harvest wheat
terror and ambition fill their stomachs
as famine drives like a snowstorm across the land

romanov
strafed and bayoneted in a basement
old paper giving way to guns and new signatures

romanov
son of woman and man
son of fallen gods
sprawled among his slaughtered children
a stone in his open hand

romanov bones clattering down a mine shaft
jewellery spattered in the mud and grass
it all comes round
these bones scattered in the earth and water
forgotten and shattered as storms rage through the cemeteries
these bones changing slowly slowly
shifting into relics
the icons of another day

✖

a monk on fire … the serenity and rage … not a sacrifice, really, a signal, a gesture … the rage of flames wrapping themselves around him, the absolute control and rage of flames flaying him alive without thought or intent, only the duty to burn and feed, wrapping themselves around him like a saffron robe, his second skin …

the horrible serenity of the human machine without desire …

a transfiguration …

out of the corner of my eye
a memory of a black wing
a slow-motion movement
something not quite there
like words say or love

the sound of wings flapping
somewhere

✖

sailboats and walkways at the forks
endless june skies and air like silk
dubrovnik maybe or a film set

a ceremony of suits and lights
a cabinet minister with scissors
cutting a red ribbon

fuck you fuck you fuck you!
yeah that's my boy

a voice from the river's edge
who cares who cares who cares?
that's my boy

there's a carnival downriver
a golden retriever strung up by its leash
a siamese dragging its broken back into a hole
there's a top hat playing solitaire on a rock

the river's alive with rats and condoms
an empty suitcase an arm a leg

glittering eyes in the underbrush
the grunt of someone getting fucked
billy graham's distant radio voice

save me save me save me
cries the princess to the frog
his long hind legs wrapped around her

a child with a hammer
looking for someone to blame

※

a shadow in the window
a voice about to speak
a sniper in my heart
and a body in the creek

a black limousine turns a corner
sun glinting off the driver's shades

a day to dream of
the unending blue sky

a child lying in grass
staring into the sky

a white cat on the riverbank
looking for mice

handshakes in the back seat
a flag fluttering on the front fender

above them a shadow balanced on the sill
of a brown window in the late afternoon

✖

not even a shadow in the window
behind the curtains
not a breath or motion
as if he's part of the wall
a drawing or mural

at the precise moment
the blond boy slows at the intersection
a shape lifts swiftly off the wall
a man and a rifle with telescopic sight
suddenly a human with features
there in the vacant window
a split-second shot
and only a shivering curtain left behind

bluebeard in the shadows
the groom of dreams

some women yearn
for bluebeard
on a late saturday night
once a year
loving his danger
and his impersonal eyes

bluebeard the wild
knowing what he wants
and taking it

bluebeard the shadow groom
who will marry you in the grave

※

on the city's broad avenue
an elegant horse on parade
like a warkov painting
crowds drifting past the shops

crippled children watch from the curb
newspapers swirling around their feet
there is a weeping face at each window
and dogs baying behind the wall

the horse plods through the streets
drawing a hearse behind it
peasant women cross themselves
muttering prophecies

the procession carries a king to his tomb
heavy clouds draping the city
the people go silent and the riders pause
waiting for the rain

✠

an assassin's mask fallen
at the scene of the crime
the great hall of mirrors
and he can't be found
in the crowd

a second mask slides to the floor
like a whisper of paper
and then another and another
the floor is littered with masks
and none of the assassins can be found

a brilliant disguise
the mask removed
an impossible puzzle for the police
everyone looked alike at first
and now they look alike again

a moment later they are at each other
each and every person in the crowd
with drawn knives and snub-nosed pistols
like a battle scene from the middle ages
close quarters and jousting

and when it's over
they're on all fours
looking for their masks
and silently turning
toward their lives

✖

a woman in the attic
thumbs through old magazines
looking for her true love

she remembers his eyes
how he yearned for her
as she yearned for him
she remembers his arms around her
the cologne on his smooth cheeks
she remembers everything
how he combed his hair
with his head at a slant
how he laughed with delight
when she hung his photo on the wall
and in her own hand
signed it *with all my love elvis*

❂

from estrus to romance
from romance to coltrane
man and woman
contending in the rain

ah love
byzantine exaltation
all icons and worship
an addiction to paradise
and the end of time
the grease of serotonim
slippery in the brain

then turn around
and a numbing despair
the machine collapsed
into nuts and bolts and pain
and no sense anywhere
the music broken
and time dragging its ass
across a field of shattered glass

two of us
walking in the rain
sodden clothes
clinging to these bodies
of skin and brain and heart
and all the other parts
lust and love
the betrayal
and the companion you've always dreamed

from estrus to romance
what a waltz
how the earth accumulates
its wars and fossils
how we keep digging them up
and falling in love

the words to a lullabye keep recurring
the clicking of train wheels
old casey and the orange blossom special
on its way to the end of the line

swing the pick
tote that load

old songs at memory's edge
the old moon in the new moon's arms
a dead knight beneath his shield

the words that sang me to sleep
on the tip of my tongue
and me dreaming in the quarry
an endless line of shuffling figures
trains lumbering by
swollen with freight
and nothing but the clicking of wheels

⊗

I am malory the rapist imaginer of romance and chivalry inventor of the world you play at you will find me beneath the bridge with a blade in hand throw me your paltry coins or I will run you through

I am torquemada your personal confessor I will guide you to heaven I am the duke of alva let me invite you to holocaust everyone will be there

I am savanarola and john calvin come warm yourself at my fire we'll talk about your doubts I'm sure I have an answer

I am marco polo I am prester john I've been everywhere and I come from nowhere that you know I could tell you things you would never believe so I tell you things you will believe I'm waiting for you at the end of your quest

I am the ripper the first true terrorist artist extraordinaire I express myself personally with truth and precision I am your aesthetic

I am raskolnikov the sensitive the bored living in my head where society never comes never cares I am sorrowful raskolnikov existential decider of fates society's executioner

I live in your neighbourhood lizzie borden lingering behind frilly curtains florence bravo with her domestic poisons and spice I am the family doctor in your basement hunched in the red glow of the furnace unloading a wheelbarrow full of limbs

I am your family your son and your daughter we are so close so close we hardly know each other's fantasies and despairs I am your family nightmare the suicide and slaughter the frenzy of the vast emptiness inside four walls I am the family of utter strangers each one longing for a kiss

I am the killer with his maul waiting behind the door a silhouette at your window I am the monster you dream with your secret name

※

*I am bluebeard in the shadows the groom of your dreams give me a chance
to turn my life around everyone needs love let me crawl into your arms
mama let me suck your tit let me come home*

*I am the woman who wants to succumb for a moment to the kisses and
blows of a dangerous man I want to be taken into orgasm and forgetting I
want the thrill of flirtation in the shadows I want to betray someone even if
it's me*

✖

*there are a million people who lust for the permission of mirrors the freedom
to watch themselves making love*

*like the photographs your grandfather took of the family gathered around
an open casket*

seeing is believing

make real make real make real

a broken dish
a spoon

on a vase
an obliterated body
with reaching graceful arms

bones scattered
around a fire

✖.

their broken streets and walls
their laws their children's rage
the cities are dying
yearning for the fire
crying for an end to things

where are the tribes
those on foot
the lean ones from the desert?
where are the lost ones
to destroy our cities?

where is the mau mau
with his oath
ghosting through the trees?
where is auca despair
erupting on a river's bank?

the old stone clans
in forests and deserts
are turning to leave us
like the jaguar people
in search of the beginning of time

you can still smell them
on the paths where they passed
you can hear the distant song
of women trilling like blackbirds

you want to run and discover them again
you want to hold them close and wonder
like not quite recognizing someone in a family photograph
like scenting something familiar but gone

will they find their origins and not return?
have they left behind an ambush
a naked patrol to remind us
with arcing spears
that we have left our bodies behind?

a dish
stone steps
a dancer

scattered in grass
buried in deserts
these things of man and woman
an obsidian blade
a painted wall
these things
made us gods
in our own right

an ancient breastbone
ribs
held a fire
and let go
the contagious heart

spreading
through valleys
of the rift
the serengeti
himalayas

a disease
to make us gods
beasts in love
and war
turning to watch
the infected sky

the world going down
around us

wordless they emerge from forest and desert
clothed in the steaming skins of animals
dancing slowly into an eyeless fury

only memory can offer such rage
children broken on the wheel
their tents slashed open to the sky

⊗

going down
earth's diary
its broken bowl
and ashes

going down
through shell and leaf
and debris
to initials on the stairs

going down
the ladder
breaking into
an empty house

going down
to the world's mouth
for an echo
of the first orphan

going down
in an easy death
a raw word
in the star's cave

✠

this place of evidence

laid out bones
and the stone seeds of wreaths

the debris of home
a broken bowl
a doorstone

and a stick
with carved shapes
a calendar
or worship
a poem

this place
where a woman understood
soil and sun and moon
and stood back

someone saying
with hands
and stuttering tongue

a man turning
to look back
where he was

becoming strangers

✖

where is the desert warrior?
the city groans with anxiety
who will deliver us from misery?
from our small laws and Gods?
from the disease we wallow in?
from our schools and work lines?
who will bring fire from the desert?

�֍

going down at the digging
through bone and stone
through the memory of flesh
going down
looking for something
a flake or shard
going down
for a word
something that tells
of abiding sorrow

all the silt and cinders say
the raspings of a child
abandoned
first orphan of the world

�֎

a smouldering city
an army
glittering beneath the sun

a mediterranean dream
of words and blood
bodies aflame
impaled children
shabby gods
calculations and law

a mediterranean dream
of senators and emperors

⊗

going down
for bric-a-brac
the splinters
shaken down
through the years

going down
for stone gestures
a dance
the mouth's poem
stunned into scrawl

going down
for the pearl
the tongue
flicking across
a chasm

✖

mau mau campsite 1954

a magazine
two rifles
a bowl of blood
a monkey's bones
six sleepers
a dying fire

◈

it could have been
lhasa
an african ridge
the banks
of the curaray

born yesterday
or tomorrow
in a thatched hut
a back alley
or a muscle from the oily sea

woven
bone and blood
out of conceptions
and murders
and words
and

unknown mothers
and vanished fathers
moments
of mind and heart
forgotten
forgotten

a queen
with a brooch at her throat
sailing through death
forever
a mauled hunter
in a cave
a child
strangled in birth
bones
and dust
and earth's memory
remains

the fearful naming
of these few people
these clans
that contribute nothing
they only live
these *huaorani*
named *auca*
by their enemies
named *the savage ones*

and named by missionaries
the auca man
who crosses the river
named
like some next-door neighbor
george
the young woman
with her naked brown limbs
delilah

in the forest
their clearing
with thatched shelters
their home
named
terminal city

and the beach
where the plane lands
the beach
where for a moment
time collides
named
palm beach

☒

auca stands still
in the rain
sucking the marrow
from a bone

he's laughing
telling his only story
how he wounded an enemy
with his lance

near him
is a palm roof
but he stands there
naked in the rain

auca eruption 1956

warriors erupting from the jungle
missionaries retreating into the river
their radio and airplane stranded on the beach

young white men
knee-deep in the curaray
arms outstretched
shirttails fluttering
calling on jesus

cool water on his legs
he's remembering a classroom
with its chemistry and mathematics
his finger poised above a whirling globe
the colors of continents and oceans
the shapes of geography flashing by
standing there above the world
his finger stabbing at the globe
this is where I'll live

running downriver
his ears pounding with someone's breath
it was some other place
it must have been somewhere else
water splaying slow and silver around him
his far-away voice sounding toward heaven

a naked man pivots
and flings his lance into the future

※

the archaeologist works
where the gate of the city once stood

a slaughter he says so many bones
and yet no knives or arrow heads

he measures and sifts and calculates
making a novel with his tools
and in the end with his imagination

the city defeated he says by thirst and hunger
its inhabitants impaled outside the wall

a familiar story
I've uncovered five or six myself
it's how things were done
a tidying up of loose ends

※

then in each death
the dying away of world
a memory of water
and what's left
the voice
a grunt of discovery or pain
a shift in tone
a laugh
the ear remembering
the tongue
words suddenly in the world
amidst gestures
the voice crying inarticulately
a shout
the tongue hammering
open the planet
into poverty and wealth
into poems and equations and love
the voice
a song
from voice to voice
the song
wind in the wheat
on the cemetery grass

palm beach

what was left behind:
a stripped airplane
time magazine
with general motors' curtice
man of the year
on the cover
an overturned can of beans
stinking to high heaven
mustard
spanish new testament
wedding ring
diary
watch
auca lances
pulled from dead bodies
four bodies in the river
one caught in underwater branches
or a fallen tree
the fifth having floated away
during the night
camera found
on river bottom
etc.

✖

the last two frames
from nate saint's camera
found in the curaray

two naked women
on the beach
the curaray running
behind them
the younger one
holds a drink
and a cloth
in front of her breasts
her left leg lifted
and inclined inward
to hide her pubic hair

water has bled
like a black flame
into the next frame
and like a black flame
burned
up the middle of the frame
corroding the women
from the scene
in the background
around the black flame
trees
and always the river

auca campsite 1960

an aluminum pot
filled with white rice
a half-eaten hamburger
on a stone
a bible
a tape recorder
and a microphone

graduation 1963

roasting wieners
over a bonfire
willie's transistor
wandering
on and off the station
the trashmen singing
papa oo mau mau
papa oo mau mau

fingers
and buttons
the smell
of ripe apples
the bird is the word

bottles
glittering
near the fire
a flash bulb
freezes the night
papa oo mau mau

the fall of 63
and there's no one
in the photo
everyone's making out
or drinking
among the rocks
and trees
nothing but the garbage
of a wiener roast
and the trashmen
singing
papa oo mau mau
papa oo mau mau

and there
where desert meets the city
in a shantytown
where squalor defines our wealth
there
where God lies beneath rubble
where the bowl is broken
there
a moment we might miss
a glance
a caressing hand

you never know

✠

there is no time for this these considerations of blasphemy

thoughts in your car as you speed down highway 59 past ile des chenes worries and anxieties love having packed its bags once again no job in sight and your body shrivelling toward old man children knifing each other on the street clans and nations at each other's throats water earth and air putrefying toward apocalypse

no time for memory family or words all baggage in an overstuffed suitcase and believe me you'll be travelling light

on the other hand time is all you have and the daily blasphemy of time human stirring the restless spirit in its sheath of flesh the sorrow and pleasure of ear eye and hand the air washing across your skin

I am the boatman baling the river into his boat

I am the rooster crowing the night down

✠

A meditation on the word fuck how it is many things a curse a blessing a crutch the sound of it when spat out something angry and filthy something intimate and passionate a song when spoken with love

tranquillity of flames
like a lotus on the street
the smell of gasoline
a buddha's smile

✠

who would venture from these brutal streets to build a sacred city?
who would enter the wilderness to wear the shawl of love?

an exhausted world
someone coughing behind the door

tire slicks on the asphalt
wipers lashing at the rain

who would crawl from disease and kiss the plague goodbye?
who would walk a mile with death and leave a smile behind?

grey thistles in the cemetery
water guttering down the curb

planks across the window
newspapers waiting beneath a brick

who would embrace a god and give up the ghost?
who would walk to the river to drown?

the inconsolable spirit always on its way
the restless ghosts we are on portage avenue

should I turn in this doorway?
will the light change before I get to it?

wondering where father is
now he's been dead some twenty years

haven't read a love story in years
haven't met an old-fashioned heart

the word grows sadder every day
or is that me?

the song is everything
each song
a stone a tree
the old woman laughing on the porch
the song
singing through the dream

at the river's edge
you can dream
of the dancer

the bearded savior
disappearing into the rain

you can remember
old steps
and the human gesture

a hand waving

what startles you
is the imp
in the underbrush
doubled-over
with laughter

no
there is no easy word
for this
how we hear
for a moment
then go deaf

imagining whispers
at the river's edge

a family
gathering
in the open
and predators
slipping
through the grass

one of us
finding a way
to the end of the world
baffled there
and turning back
toward the story

a hand waving farewell
and the laughter
time and again

sometimes
you can hear the howling of their dogs
bells and the soughing wind

moving along the way
by foot or horseback

with their golden bracelets
walking past wall and plough

in long grass
they pitch their black tents
and the story begins again

✖

rain fell for a week clouds low and dark and bulging the creeks and rivers
rose and flowed as in the old days and cattle and sheep were swept away
on a roof floating downriver a dog howled at the hidden moon trees
swaying and uprooted a black shoe bobbing in the torrent

in the moonlight a hat floating downriver
shadows embracing in the underbrush
someone's singing on the bridge
I have to believe it's love

✖

only a boy
a bare body
caught in long grass
beneath the water
a drowned boy
a vanished boy
swaying inside the flood

after a week
the river released him
and slowly
silent as forgetting
drew him home

going upriver
poling through reeds
heading for the still pool
beneath the weeping willow
the place of the unborn
where invisible mouths moan
and bones collapse among the wheelchairs

a place of the slaughtered
the unlucky unwanted
crooked limbs and humped backs
short-circuits and chemical mistakes
the unborn scars of greedy dreams

a song here
of detritus
among the reeds
a red-winged blackbird

they rise from kissing the stone
they dream of fish and water
this is our cradle
we have been rocked in its sand
sometimes we hear it at our doors
whispering in our sleep
and these people rising from the stone
riders who know every hidden well

this is the only war
desert and green islands
they will come for us
as surely as the deadly sun rises
they will claim our squalid rivers
and we will return with them
to our wisdom
the desert where the dream lives

✼

there's a stranger from memory
riding a dark horse
it's the stranger who changes words
to shake off chains

there's a stranger in your clothes
ranting at the judge
it's the stranger who calls for a bolt
to split the bench

there's a stranger at your door
looking for his clan
it's the stranger who will bring down
relentless rain

there is nothing left
no more sorrow in the land

shaking off the sadness
biting into a fig
man and woman
children of earth

a smile behind the laughter
hands and lips and feet

this won't be done again
it's over

✖.

well fuck

I'll speak
I speak
out of this rack of meat
talking raw

a breath
a torn shoe

this song

✼

the recurring scene
a body half in the river
one shoe untied
a bullet hole in the head

the unprepared man
the woman on her way home
the innocent body
clothed in violence

something to remember
without a voice
there is no memory

scavenging for basho
in the mountains
someone passing through

⊗

hope?

the table overturned
and dishes falling

cities gnawing
at their own bones

flayed

and shedding the earth
our flesh

hope is not a question
it's hardly a word

but yes yes
because we are what we are
and we look ahead and talk
because we are mistaken
and blunder on

hope

that somewhere
sun-blanched
amongst the wreckage
something clean
something still left
some last good in us

a moment of sorrow
in our disarray
in this dying grace
of matter

the usual crockery

Patrick Friesen lives in Vancouver. He has written for film, radio, television and theatre. His latest book, *Blasphemer's Wheel: Selected and New Poems* won the McNally-Robinson Manitoba Book of the Year Award in 1994.